A GUIDE TO
GLOUCESTER DOCKS

HUGH CONWAY JONES

ALAN SUTTON
1988

ALAN SUTTON PUBLISHING
BRUNSWICK ROAD · GLOUCESTER

First published 1988

The selection of material for this guide is based on the experience of members of
Gloucester Civic Trust who have shown thousands of visitors around the docks.

By the same author:
   Gloucester Docks — An Illustrated History.

British Library Cataloguing in Publication Data

Conway-Jones, Hugh.
A guide to Gloucester Docks.
1.   Gloucestershire. Gloucester. Docks to 1983
I.   Title
387.1'5

ISBN 0–86299–487–X

Typesetting and origination by
Alan Sutton Publishing Limited.
Printed in Great Britain by
The Guernsey Press Company Limited,
Guernsey, Channel Islands.

Building the Canal

For hundreds of years, the River Severn provided an important trade route between the Midlands and the great port of Bristol, and many types of cargoes were carried in both directions by shallow draught sailing vessels known as trows. In 1580 Gloucester was given the formal status of a port by a charter from Elizabeth I, and a custom house was built adjoining the riverside Quay. However, few sea-going ships came up to Gloucester because of the difficulty of navigating the narrow winding river approaching the city, and even the local trows could only pass this stretch for a few days each fortnight on the spring tides.

During the eighteenth century, there was a considerable growth in trade on the river, and this led to a proposal to construct a ship canal between Gloucester and Berkeley Pill. The canal would not only allow through traffic to avoid the worst part of the river, it would also help to develop the port of Gloucester as a rival to Bristol.

The Gloucester and Berkeley Canal was authorised by Act of Parliament in 1793, and work started at the Gloucester end under the direction of Robert Mylne. Progress was slow due to the use of small inefficient contractors, poor supervision and appalling weather conditions. Also, costs increased due to the effects of the Napoleonic War, and by 1799 most of the original share capital had been spent. The basin at Gloucester was complete, but work on the canal was stopped with the digging having only progressed south as far as Hardwicke, about five miles from Gloucester.

For the next few years, there was much discussion about how the canal could be completed, but it was not possible to raise the necess-ary money. After the Napoleonic War was over, the Canal Company obtained the support of the Excheq-uer Bill Loan Commissioners, who were set up by the Government to finance schemes that would help to reduce post-war unemployment. The Company agreed to adopt a new line joining the Severn at Sharpness Point, and work started again in 1817. The project then came under the general supervision of Thomas Telford, acting as consultant engineer to the Loan Commissioners.

Construction work progressed steadily, and in 1820 a junction was made with the Stroudwater Canal, which with other waterways gave an inland route through to London. The remaining section of canal to Sharpness was delayed due to more money troubles, but then the work made good progress with a new contractor, Hugh McIntosh, working under the supervision of a new resident engineer, Thomas Fletcher, and the canal was eventually completed in 1827.

Early Use of the Basin

Severn trows using the Main Basin before the canal was completed (*Gloucester City Library*)

While the digging of the canal was halted at Hardwicke, a horse-operated railway was constructed to link the dock basin with Cheltenham, and the lock was brought into use in 1812. This allowed the basin to be used by trows bringing Forest of Dean coal up the river from Lydney and Bullo Pill, and also by boats bringing timber and roadstone from further down the estuary.

When work on the canal went ahead again, there was concern that the basin at Gloucester would not be large enough for the trade expected, and so an additional Barge Arm was constructed to ensure that the main basin could be kept free for sea-going ships. In addition to this the Canal Company built a warehouse at the north end of the basin. The canal was formally opened on the 26 April 1827, and a huge crowd gathered to watch the first two vessels enter the basin amid the firing of guns and the ringing of church bells.

Once the canal was fully operational, local merchants were soon taking advantage of the new facilities. Importing through Gloucester cut out the former need for transhipment at Bristol, where there were high port charges. Cargoes could be transferred direct to canal longboats which could carry the goods up the river and through the inland canals to supply the growing industrial towns of the Midlands.

The geographical position of

Gloucester so far inland was a tremendous advantage, and traffic was soon exceeding all expectations. As well as the trows and barges employed in the river and coastal trade, there were increasing numbers of two-masted brigs and schooners and some three-masted barques. Early imports included corn from Ireland and the Continent, timber from the Baltic and North America, and wines and spirits from Portugal and France. The main export was salt which was brought down the river from Worcestershire.

To cope with all this activity, warehouses were built around the Main Basin, an earlier dry dock was enlarged, and an engine house was built to augment the canal's water supply by pumping from the River Severn. To extend the quay space, Bakers Quay was constructed along the canal, and this was mainly laid out for timber yards. Large storage yards were necessary as the timber loading ports were iced-up during the winter and most of the imports arrived during the summer and autumn. Several of the yards were surrounded by high fences and were locked up under customs supervision so that foreign timber could be stored there without paying import duty. Some of the vessels bringing timber from North America were locally owned, and they often carried emigrants on the outward journey.

The approach to the docks in 1843. Bakers Quay and the Pillar Warehouse are on the right and the original wooden Llanthony Bridge is on the left (*Gloucester City Library*)

Development of the Docks

The lock between the Main Basin and the river in 1850 (*Gloucester City Library*)

During the 1840s, it was realised that further developments would be necessary. At busy times, the basin became so crowded that vessels had to wait their turn for a berth. Also, there was a national movement towards reduced import duties, and particularly following the repeal of the Corn Laws in 1846, the Canal Company recognised they should prepare for a major increase in foreign imports. They therefore arranged for the Victoria Dock to be constructed to the east of the Main Basin with a narrow cut linking the two, and the new dock was opened in 1849. At the same time, further corn warehouses were built and new timber yards were established.

Also during the 1840s, there were various moves to bring rail-way connections into the docks. Initially, improvements were made to the existing horse-operated line, but this was still unsatisfactory due to its narrow gauge and sharp bends. Then the Midland Railway constructed a standard gauge line from their station to the south end of Bakers Quay with a branch serving the east side of the main docks area. A few years later, the Gloucester and Dean Forest Railway built a branch from the South Wales line to serve a new quay on the west side of the canal, and this was operated by the Great Western Railway. These lines were increasingly used to distribute imports to the Midlands in competition with the river and canal route.

With the benefit of the improved

facilities, foreign imports increased dramatically during the 1850s and 60s. Corn came from northern Europe and the Black Sea ports situated around the mouth of the Danube, further warehouses were constructed and three flour mills were established. Timber came from the Baltic, North America and the arctic coast of Russia, and new timber yards and saw mills were established beside the canal south of Gloucester. Other imports included wines and spirits, oranges and lemons, and bones and guano for fertiliser. Unfortunately, salt was still the only regular export, and most vessels had to go elsewhere to find a return cargo.

Around the middle of the nineteenth century, many wooden sailing ships were built at Gloucester, the main yard being to the south-west of the Main Basin. With the advent of iron and steel vessels being built elsewhere, however, the local industry declined.

During the 1860s, difficulties were reported because the general increase in the size of merchant ships meant that some were too big to come up the canal fully laden. The Canal Company therefore built a new entrance and dock at Sharpness that would take the largest ships of the day. The new dock opened in 1874, and this allowed the growth in imports to continue. The smaller boats came up the canal as before, whilst cargoes from the larger vessels were transhipped at Sharpness and brought up the canal in barges and lighters.

Looking south across the Main Basin in 1883 (*Gloucester City Library*)

Changes in Traffic

Goods being transferred from a barge to a longboat to be taken on to Birmingham *c.* 1910 (*A. Thomas*)

By the early years of this century, the docks were being used by steamers as well as by sailing vessels, and there were regular services to continental ports. However, the continuing increase in the size of merchant ships, particularly steamers, meant that a growing proportion of the goods coming to Gloucester arrived in barges and lighters from Sharpness or other Bristol Channel ports. Much of the corn was sent straight on to the Midlands, and this led to a decline in the use of the warehouses at Gloucester.

During the 1920s, a new traffic was generated by the demand for petroleum products for the growing number of road vehicles with internal combustion engines. This became very important in the years following, and a fleet of tanker barges was used to bring the petroleum from Avonmouth. Some of the barges continued up the river to depots at Worcester and Stourport.

Unfortunately, the growth in road transport brought to an end the operation of two passenger steamers which had provided a regular service along the canal since the 1850s. *The Wave* and *The Lapwing* were used by villagers coming to shop in Gloucester and by townspeople wanting a pleasant day out, but they could not compete when the faster motor buses became established.

The old Canal Company was nationalised in 1947, and the new management set about encouraging more sea-going ships to come up to Gloucester. The docks also remained busy with barge traffic well into the 1960s. The petroleum traffic then declined rapidly following the construction of underground pipelines and the establishment of a depot at Quedgeley, and the other barge traffic came to an end in the face of competition from road transport. By 1980, virtually the only remaining commercial vessels were the coasters coming to the quays south of Llanthony Bridge.

As the commercial traffic died away, it was partly replaced by an increase in pleasure craft, and the docks became a popular place for moorings. The survival of the old warehouses made the Main Basin an ideal location for filming historical drama, and many scenes for the popular television series *The Onedin Line* were filmed in front of Biddles Warehouse. Also, a company owning square-rigged ships established their base in the docks, and their vessels have been featured in many other television series and films.

Much has now changed as the docks have taken on a new role to suit modern needs, but there is still much of interest to be seen, and the remainder of this guide provides the historical background to the main features. The photographs were taken in the 1980s before the major redevelopments. A map is provided on the centre page to identify the location of places referred to. Visitors are reminded that the docks are private property and not all parts are accessible.

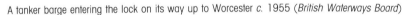

A tanker barge entering the lock on its way up to Worcester *c.* 1955 (*British Waterways Board*)

The Main Basin

View across the Main Basin from the large dry dock. The North Warehouse is supported by scaffolding prior to restoration

The Main Basin was constructed between 1794 and 1799 by gangs of men working only with spades and wheelbarrows. The barrows were wheeled over lines of planks, and the earth was tipped out to build up the surrounding land, particularly the bank by the river. The work was hampered by some very severe winters, and the excavation was flooded on more than one occasion. It was a major undertaking for its time, and it is perhaps not surprising that five successive contractors were employed before the work was completed.

After the canal was opened in 1827, the Basin became increasingly busy with ships from all over the world, and some had to moor in the middle while waiting for a spare berth. During the nineteenth century, sailing vessels predominated, and their magnificent masts often towered above the warehouses. In this century steamers became more common and then motor vessels, but now the commercial traffic has gone and the basin is mainly used by pleasure craft.

Around the walls of the Basin can be seen the safety chains to aid anyone who falls into the water. The earliest chains were installed in the 1870s after many cases of sailors drowning while returning, often the worse for drink, to their ships in the dark.

The Victoria Dock

The Victoria Dock was opened in 1849 to accommodate the growth in imports following the repeal of the Corn Laws. From the start, it was served by sidings from the newly-completed Midland Railway line into the docks. The entrance cut from the Main Basin was originally crossed only by a footbridge, and the present Victoria Bridge is a later installation built to inprove the railway system in the docks.

The Victoria Dock was also known as the Salt Basin, as this was where salt from Droitwich and Stoke Prior was transferred to sea-going ships for Ireland and the Continent. Small schooners collected salt here until the early 1940s. Commercial traffic continued for another twenty years, but now the dock has become a marina.

The Albert Warehouse was converted to a flour mill in 1869, a boiler house was built to the south and other buildings were added later. In 1880 the mill was the first in the district to have roller milling machines installed, and the manager became famous for the evening classes he organised for others to learn the new techniques. The mill continued operating until 1977, when the equipment was stripped out and the ancilliary buildings demolished. Later the warehouse became the home of the Robert Opie Collection illustrating a century of retail packaging.

The Victoria Dock with barges formerly used for bringing wheat to the City Flour Mills. Beyond (from left to right) are the Llanthony, Albert and Britannia Warehouses – the latter gutted by fire on 1 April 1987

The City Flour Mills

The City Flour Mills with the original building on the right, the warehouse in the centre and a modern silo on the left. The gantry was used to bring in wheat from a suction intake plant beside the Victoria Dock

The mill dates from 1850 and is an early example of the gradual movement of the industry from water-powered sites in the country to steam-powered mills at the ports. The original plant consisted of a few pairs of stones and some flour dressing machines driven by a steam engine. The venture was so successful that it was soon necessary to build the adjoining warehouse and add more plant.

Since 1886 the mill has been run by Priday Metford and Co., an independent family firm that supplies bakeries over a wide area. Soon after they took over, the warehouse was badly damaged by a spectacular fire, but fortunately the mill itself was not seriously affected and they were soon back in business. The slightly different brick used in the rebuilding can still be seen.

There have been numerous changes to the mill since then, replacing and updating the plant which now comprises roller milling machinery powered by electricity. The wheat used to be brought by barges to a suction intake plant beside the Victoria Dock, but now it comes by road, mainly from English farms.

The Dock Office

The original building was the office of the Gloucester and Berkeley Canal Company, which was responsible for operating the canal and for developing the docks. The building also included living accommodation for the Company's clerk. Following nationalisation of the Canal Company, the office was used by the British Waterways Board. A plaque on the wall commemorates the visit of the Duke of Gloucester to a boat rally in 1980 celebrating the 400th anniversary of the charter which established the port of Gloucester.

Opposite the office is a reconstructed doorway which formerly led into the Docks Coffee House. This was established in 1877 by the Chaplain of the Mariners Chapel to provide the dock workers with a cheap alternative to beer. Sandwiches and cocoa were provided as well as coffee, and a rowing boat was used to take refreshment round to the ships and to the men working in the timber yards down the canal. The nearby drinking fountain was provided by the Local Board of Health in 1863 as previously there had been no public supply in the docks. It was intended for the dock workers, but it was sometimes monopolised by sailors filling water casks for their ships.

The former office of the Gloucester and Berkeley Canal Company

The North Warehouse

The warehouse is of particular importance as it was the first to be built, and it served as a model for all those that followed. It was built by the Gloucester and Berkeley Canal Company and was completed just in time for the opening of the canal in 1827. Its siting was recommended by Thomas Telford, who was supervising the completion of the canal, and the detailed design was provided by Bartin Haigh, a Liverpool builder who had probably had experience of constructing dock warehouses in his home town.

The bricks used for the walls probably came from the riverside brickworks at Walham, and the stone sills and lintels came from Bath and the Forest of Dean. The timber for the roof frames and the floors was probably imported from the Baltic, and the roof slates were brought round the coast from North Wales. The cast-iron columns supporting the floors most likely came from William Montague's foundry near Westgate Bridge. A stone tablet near the top of the front wall is inscribed 'The Glocester and Berkeley Canal Company's Warehouses Erected by W. Rees and Son Ano. Dom. 1826'.

The upper part of the building was designed so that individual floors on each side of the central partition wall could be rented to different merchants. There were two sets of boxed-in stairs with lockable doors on all floors, so that each merchant only had access to his own goods and to the hoisting winches that were installed in the roof space over the loading doors. The early tenants were mainly local

The North Warehouse converted into offices for Gloucester City Council

merchants who started importing wheat, barley and oats from Ireland and from Europe, and the brick-vaulted cellars were used for storing wines and spirits imported from Portugal and France. Later, floors were mainly rented by larger merchants who had their own warehouses but still used part of the Canal Company's building for additional space when required. In the present century, the whole building was occupied by Priday Metford and Co., who operated the nearby City Flour Mills, and in one half they installed an electric-powered mill for producing stoneground wheatmeal flour. They moved out in 1962, and then the condition of the building was allowed to deteriorate.

A proposal for demolition was resisted, and eventually the City Council bought the building for £1 and set about making it suitable for their main offices. Most of the roof had to be replaced, but the main timbers were retained wherever possible. Any woodwork that had been affected by rot was cut away and replaced by short metal girders. The former loading doors on each floor were replaced by windows, and the brick vaulting of one of the cellars was destroyed to allow the introduction of a lift shaft and staircase. The uprights and wires supporting the entrance porches were inspired by the masts and rigging of the old sailing ships. The restoration work, completed in July 1986, successfully provided a pleasant working environment for the Council staff whilst still retaining the main features of the original warehouse. It also set an example which helped to stimulate the major redevelopment of the docks and the restoration of all the other warehouses.

The former ship's bell on the corner of the warehouse used to be rung by a watchman to signal the dockers' starting and finishing times. It also served occasionally as an alarm bell when there was a fire on board a ship or in a warehouse. In the 1940s the bell was installed on a light tower at Shepperdine as a navigation aid during foggy conditions on the Severn estuary. It was re-erected by the Rotary Club of Gloucester and the Gloucester Civic Trust to mark the restoration of the North Warehouse. The adjoining sign painted on the east end of the building is a renovation of a sign dating from the 1880s.

On the quay in front of the warehouse are remnants of the former dock railway system and some large stones that once formed the foundations of a manually-operated crane.

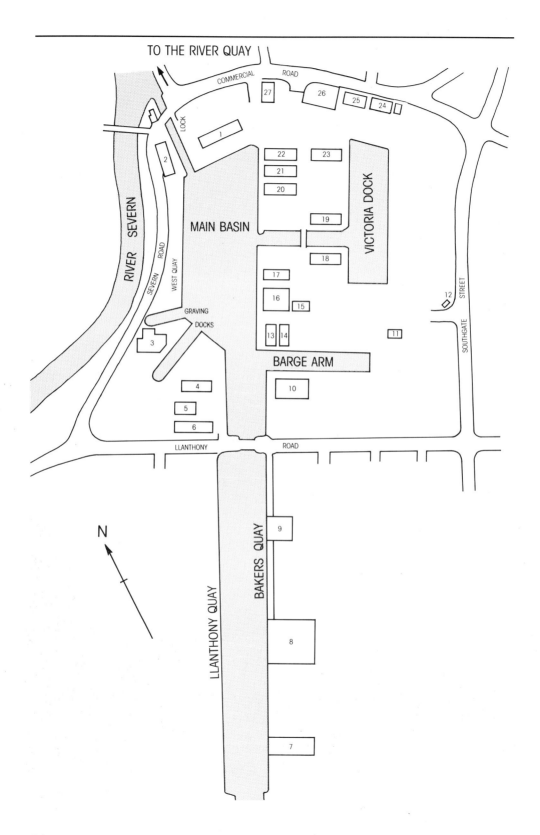

TO THE RIVER QUAY

COMMERCIAL ROAD

27   26   25   24

LOCK

1

2

22   23

21

20

RIVER SEVERN

SEVERN ROAD

WEST QUAY

MAIN BASIN

19

VICTORIA DOCK

18

17

16   15

12   SOUTHGATE STREET

GRAVING DOCKS

3

13   14

11

BARGE ARM

4

10

5

6

LLANTHONY ROAD

N

9

LLANTHONY QUAY

BAKERS QUAY

8

7

1. North Warehouse (1826–7)
2. Lock Warehouse (1834)
3. Engine House (from 1834)
4. Alexandra Warehouse (1870)
5. Alexandra Kiln (1888)
6. Great Western
   Warehouse* (1863)
7. Foster Brothers
   Oil and Cake Mill (1862)
8. Downings Malt-house (1899)
9. Pillar Warehouse (c1838)
10. Llanthony Warehouse (1873)
11. Cottages
12. Weighbridge House (1849)
13. Biddles Warehouse (1830)
* Gutted by fire

14. Shiptons Warehouse (1833)
15. Mariners Chapel (1849)
16. Reynolds (or Sturges)
    Warehouse (1840)
17. Vinings Warehouse (1840)
18. Albert Warehouse (1851)
19. Britannia Warehouse* (1861)
20. Phillpotts Warehouse (1846)
21. Kimberley Warehouse (1846)
22. Herbert Warehouse (1846)
23. Victoria Warehouse (1849)
24. Offices (1848)
25. Custom House (1845)
26. City Flour Mills (from 1850)
27. Dock Office (1831)

The *Soren Larsen* being turned prior to departure

Gloucester Lock

Gloucester Lock leading from the Main Basin into the River Severn with the riverside Quay in the distance

Originally there was a double lock, and the recesses for the middle gates can still be seen. It was brought into operation in 1812 to allow some use of the basin before the canal was completed. The normal summer level of the river is about 4m below the water in the docks, but there have been times of flood when the river has risen above the level of the docks, and special flood gates are provided to protect against this.

In the nineteenth century, large numbers of boats passed through the lock carrying imported corn and timber up the river to Worcester or Stourport, and many went on through the narrow canals to Birmingham and the Black Country. The coming of the railways brought competition, and the lock was deepened in 1892 to allow the use of larger vessels which were more economic. During and after the Second World War, the lock was in regular use by tanker barges carrying up to 400 tons of petroleum products to Worcester with smaller barges going on to Stourport, but now the traffic is almost exclusively pleasure craft.

The warehouse beside the lock has large windows that were inserted earlier this century when the building was used for cleaning and repairing sacks that were hired by farmers and by merchants handling imported corn. It is now an Antiques Centre with the upper floors designed as arcades of small shops.

The River Quay

Before the docks were built, cargoes were loaded and unloaded at the riverside Quay towards the far end of the reach visible from Gloucester Lock. The Quay was mainly used by trows and barges operating up the river as far as Shrewsbury or down to Bristol and South Wales, but occasional arrivals of sea-going ships are also recorded. Behind the Quay were many small warehouses and yards for storing the cargoes being transhipped, and there were several public houses frequented by the boatmen. The only building surviving from those days is the early eighteenth-century stone-faced Custom House, which had a store-room on the ground floor and offices above.

The present stone quay wall was constructed in 1887–8, and as it was so high, it formerly had several sets of steps inset into the wall to give access to the boats moored there. Traffic on the river was severely affected by competition from the railways, but the Quay continued to be used for receiving Staffordshire coal until well into the twentieth century.

The Quay is now part of the Maritime Walk, a signposted route linking the docks and the city centre, with information plaques highlighting features of historic interest along the way.

This view of the lock can be compared with the earlier view on page 6

The Warehouses

The best view of the warehouses is obtained from the West Quay. The major warehouses are all remarkably similar in design considering that they were built for a variety of different owners over a period of almost fifty years. This uniformity of style was partly due to the Canal Company imposing conditions in the leases of the land, and partly because almost all the warehouses were built for the corn trade. Each building was usually occupied by a single merchant, but sometimes the basement was leased separately. Vast quantities of imported wheat, oats, barley, maize, beans and peas were stored in sacks until the merchant found a customer.

All the warehouses have brick walls and slate roofs, and the many small windows usually have stone lintels and cills. The window openings were as much for ventilation as for light, and they were generally fitted with wooden shutters rather than glass. Some of the warehouses have a few slightly larger windows on the ground floor which were for illuminating an office, and some even had a fireplace and chimney so that the office could be heated. By the end of the nineteenth century it had become common for occupiers to paint a name in large letters on the outside of their warehouse.

To carry the heavy sacks of corn, the floors rest on massive wooden

Warehouses along the east side of the Main Basin

beams, which usually span the whole width of the building and are supported by hollow cast-iron columns. In most of the later warehouses the columns carry the names of the local iron-founders who made them. To avoid the beams being crushed locally by loads from the columns above, solid cast-iron pins pass through holes in the beams and transmit the vertical loads directly to the columns below. In the roof space, there were manually-operated winches used for hoisting the sacks up to the required floor. These had a large brake wheel which was operated by a rope hanging down outside the building and controlled by a man standing inside the loading door being used.

Although the warehouses are so similar, some evolution in design can be observed. The early warehouses have a basement and four or five stories with a long elevation facing the dock. The later warehouses are generally larger with an extra storey, and a gable end faces the dock so that the building makes better use of the land space behind the quay. The buildings were set back from the water to allow general access to the quays, which remained the property of the Canal Company.

The Lock Warehouse originally had rather widely spaced cast-iron columns supporting the floors, and it was later found necessary to add intermediate columns and beams to provide extra support. At the same time, the lower floor was made level with the ground instead of its being about 1m above. The new columns can be identified as they carry their maker's name, and the new beams are in two overlapping halves that are bolted together.

The Alexandra Warehouse is unusual in having a parapet at the top of the walls. The roof originally had eaves like the other warehouses, but this building was badly damaged by a fire which started in the eaves, and it was subsequently rebuilt with a parapet. Another serious fire occurred at the nearby Great Western Warehouse which had been used for storing sugar, and only the ground floor was brought back into use with a new roof. The adjoining Alexandra Kiln was built as a malt-house.

On the opposite side of the basin, Biddles Warehouse is also unusual in having relatively large windows with segmental heads. The architect came from Stroud, and it seems that he followed the practice used on many of the cloth mills of that area.

There was formerly a row of early warehouses along the West Quay, but they were demolished in the 1960s. The remaining buildings are not suitable for modern warehousing, and most have stood empty for many years. Proposals for further demolition have been resisted, however, and exciting new uses are being found for these massive memorials to Victorian enterprise.

The Graving Docks

In the large graving dock is the dredger *Thomas Fletcher* and a mud hopper barge. In the centre of the picture is the former engine house with the stump of the old chimney

The old wooden sailing ships were often in need of maintenance, and so it was important to have adequate graving dock facilities where work could be done on a vessel's hull. The small graving dock was enlarged to its present size in 1837. A culvert was provided to allow water from the dock to be drained out into the river, but if the river level was high, it used to take eight men seven hours to pump the water out. The larger dock was built in 1853 to accommodate the larger vessels that were then using the canal. For this dock, a steam engine was provided to pump the water out when necessary. In recent years, both docks have been used for maintaining British Waterways Board boats and other vessels.

The Engine House was built in 1834 for a beam engine that pumped water from the River Severn to make up that lost through operation of the locks. Provision had been made to take supplies from the River Cam and other streams, but these were found to be insufficient. Regular pumping is still required because, as well as the losses through use of the locks, water is also taken from the canal at Purton to provide drinking water for Bristol. The present pumps are electric-powered, and they are usually run at night when electricity is cheaper.

The water pumped from the River Severn contains a high proportion of silt which tends to settle out in the Main Basin. This can be particularly bad during the summer months, and it usually becomes necessary to dredge the whole basin during the autumn to re-establish a depth of at least 5m. The former steam-powered dredger has been restored and is now part of the collection of the National Waterways Museum. The present dredger is named Thomas Fletcher after the resident engineer who worked with Thomas Telford on the completion of the canal. The buckets of the dredger scoop up the silt and deposit it into mud hopper barges. These are towed down the canal to Purton, where the silt is pumped back into the estuary while the tug returns with empty hoppers ready for dredging the next day.

Llanthony Bridge

The original bridge, illustrated on page 5, was made of wood in two halves which swung open separately. In 1862 a single leaf bridge was constructed to carry a railway line across the canal, and some traces of the turning mechanism can still be seen. The former bridge-keeper's house in Llanthony Road is now part of the National Waterways Museum complex.

Llanthony Bridge has to be raised even for small pleasure craft

Bakers Quay

The stretch of canal immediately south of Llanthony Bridge effectively became part of the docks as the canal was widened and quays were constructed down either side. Bakers Quay was constructed in the 1830s to ease the overcrowding in the Main Basin. It was financed by a group of local merchants and bankers at a time when the Canal Company was still heavily in debt, and it was part of the agreement with the Canal Company that any warehouses would be built with their upper stories projecting forward and supported by pillars on the quay wall. This was to allow a winch in the loft to lift goods out of a ship's hold, and at the same time to leave the quay open for public use.

Soon after the quay was completed, the Pillar Warehouse was constructed as two semi-detached units with a central dividing wall and massive 18m long timber beams supporting the floors. The remainder of Bakers Quay initially served as timber yards, and ships came from the Baltic and North America bringing rough-hewn logs, sawn deals and pieces suitable for masts, barrel staves, etc.

During the second half of the nineteenth century, more timber yards were established farther down the canal, and the land on Bakers Quay was gradually built over. Two of these buildings have their upper floors projecting forward and supported on pillars in accordance with the old agreement concerning the original construction of the quay.

The Pillar Warehouse and later buildings on Bakers Quay

Llanthony Quay

Llanthony Quay was constructed by the Gloucester and Dean Forest Railway in 1852 to provide an outlet for coal from the Forest of Dean. In the event, the rail link to the Forest mines was mainly used to distribute the coal locally, and very little was exported. The quay was more used by vessels transferring imports to the Great Western Railway, who took over operation of the goods yard behind the quay. The GWR had lines serving the west side of the docks, and they also establihsed a sheet work for making all the tarpaulins used for covering railway wagons. In later years, the Bristol Steam Navigation Company operated a regular service from Germany and Holland bringing a wide range of general cargoes, particularly sugar, and a large transit shed was constructed on the quay to hold goods waiting to go on by rail.

During the Second World War, a huge grain silo was built beyond the end of the Quay for storing and drying the large ammounts of home-grown wheat, and this is still in use. After the war, the Quay was regularly used by coasters, and the original transit shed with a raised floor was supplemented by two more sheds that were suitable for vehicular access. In 1984, however, the quay wall cracked and started to subside into the canal, so commercial traffic was transferred to the quays farther down the canal.

The transit sheds on Llanthony Quay with the grain silo beyond

Llanthony Warehouse

An artist's impression of Llanthony Warehouse as the National Waterways Museum with the former steam powered dredger (*British Waterways Board*)

Llanthony Warehouse, built in 1873, is the largest and the last of the big warehouses to be built at Gloucester. After this time, further developments were mainly around the new dock at Sharpness. The warehouse was built for the Bristol-based corn merchants Wait James & Co. who continued to use it until they went bankrupt in 1926. Later it was occupied by a firm of builders merchants, and then it stood empty for several years. There was a threat of demolition in 1971, when the quay wall in front of the warehouse moved forward and subsided into the basin, but the wall was eventually re-constructed without any adverse effects on the foundations of the warehouse.

During 1987, the building was thoroughly renovated by the British Waterways Board to become the nucleus of their National Waterways Museum. The beginnings, growth and decline of the canal system are presented with the help of original artefacts, working models, archive film and historic vessels. Alongside, a traditional canal maintenance yard has been re-created and live displays demonstrate the jobs and skills that were needed to run the canals. Much of the museum car park occupies the site of a timber yard that was in use for over one hundred and fifty years.

The Barge Arm

The Barge Arm was constructed in 1824 to provide space for smaller vessels to load and unload whilst keeping the Main Basin clear for sea-going ships. The surrounding land was divided up into nine yards on each side, and these were used by merchants handling coal, stone builders materials, etc.

Each of the yards was served by a siding of the early form of railway, known as a tramroad, that linked the docks with Cheltenham. Cast iron L-section rails were laid directly on to stone blocks, and the rails were held in place by nails driven into oak pegs inserted into a hole in each block. The wagons were pulled by horses and were particularly used to carry coal that had been brought by boat from the Forest of Dean.

In the present century the Barge Arm was the base for the boats of the Severn and Canal Carrying Company which was the major carrier by water between the Bristol Channel ports and the Midlands. Cargoes from Bristol, Avonmouth and South Wales were transhipped here from barges into longboats for distribution to Birmingham and the Black Country. Some goods were stored in Biddles and Shiptons Warehouses on the corner of the Main Basin. The firm was particularly involved with carrying cocoa beans, sugar and strawboard to Cadburys factories at Frampton, Blackpole and Bournville. One of their motor boats is in the collection of the National Waterways Museum.

The Barge Arm and the former warehouses of the Severn and Canal Carrying Company

The Mariners Chapel

The Mariners Chapel

Visiting sailors used to say that they would not attend the local parish church on Sundays because they did not have any smart clothes to wear. So money was collected to provide a chapel in the docks where sailors' clothes would not look out of place. The chapel was opened in 1849, and a full-time chaplain was appointed by the bishop. He visited each ship when it arrived, making the sailors feel welcome and distributing religious tracts in many different languages. He held regular services for the sailors and the dock workers, with some special services in foreign languages, and he ran bible classes and an adult evening school. Later a Mariners Hall and Reading Room were established in a former cheese warehouse on the corner of Southgate St. and Llanthony Rd.

The chapel is still in use, and visitors are welcome. The stained glass windows came from the old St Catharine's Church in Gloucester when this was demolished in 1921. The organ was built to commemorate the ministry of Rev. George Mallett, who was chaplain for nearly twenty years around the turn of the century. This must have been played by the poet Ivor Gurney, organist here for a time before he experienced the horrors of the First World War.

The Docks Entrance

By the docks entrance in Southgate St. are two nineteenth-century cottages that were built for employees of the Canal Company. Just outside the entrance is the former weighbridge house which was contemporary with the Victoria Dock and echoes the style of the bridge-keepers' houses along the canal.

The Custom House

The Custom House which faces on to Commercial Road was designed by Sidney Smirke and was opened in 1845. It was well sited to monitor the huge expansion in foreign trade that took place during the second half of the nineteenth century. The customs officers recorded cargoes being imported and exported and collected the appropriate duties. They also kept a register of all the ships belonging to the port, and they checked on the seamen's terms and conditions of employment.

The building now houses the museum of the Gloucestershire Regiment, which has won battle honours over almost three centuries of service to Crown and Country. The collection includes uniforms, weapons, medals and pictures from battles fought in every part of the world. Farther up Commercial Road is a block of offices built for merchants trading in the docks.

The Custom House in Commercial Road

Down the Canal

The former Downings Malt-house (left) and Foster Brothers Oil and Cake Mill (right) viewed from Abbey Rd

To complete a full impression of the docks at Gloucester, it is necessary to go a little way down the canal. The best views are obtained from a boat, but some features of interest can be seen from Abbey Rd off Hempsted Lane, from the Madleaze Industrial Estate off Bristol Rd and from Hempsted Bridge.

At the south end of Bakers Quay is a former oil and cake mill, established by Foster Brothers in 1862, where imported linseed and cotton seed was crushed to give oil and the residue was sold for cattle food. To the north, Downings Malt-house was built in 1899 as an extension to an earlier building in Merchants Rd. Between them, on the site of the High Orchard Dock was the goods yard of the Midland Railway which operated the lines serving the east side of the docks.

Farther south are the former premises of the Gloucester Wagon Works. This was started in 1860 to manufacture railway wagons, and production later included carriages and road vehicles as well. The firm became one of Gloucester's largest employers and exported their products all over the world. The premises are now occupied by a trading estate.

On the west side of the canal is Monk Meadow Dock, which was constructed in 1892 to provide more facilities for the timber trade. The modernised transit shed on the south side was originally an aircraft hangar which was re-erected here soon after the First World War. In the 1920s, the dock began to be used to handle petroleum products, and several oil companies erected storage tanks. A large fleet of motor barges brought petrol and oil from Avonmouth, and some went on up the river to depots at Worcester and Stourport. This traffic declined in the 1970s following the construction of underground pipelines, and the dock was later used by coasters. Coasters also came to Monk Meadow Quay, constructed in 1965 along the canal to the south, but this traffic has declined too.

On the east side of the canal, there were formerly timber yards stretching almost all the way from the Wagon Works to Hempsted Bridge. Some of these yards were developed during the 1840s and 1850s when huge quantities of wood were imported from the Baltic and North America for use in constructing railways. To unload the ships, men carried individual pieces of wood on their shoulders while running along lines of planks to where the particular size of wood was being stacked, and then they ran back for more.

Coasters in Monk Meadow Dock viewed from the Madleaze Industrial Estate

A few of the yards still exist, and the chimneys of the associated saw mills can still be seen, but most of the timber now arrives by road. The long-established firm of Price Walker & Co. once had a canal frontage of a quarter of a mile, and they claimed to be the biggest softwood importers in the country. Part of their yard is now occupied by the Permali factory, but a remnant of their gantry crane still survives on the side of the canal.

Approaching Hempsted Bridge, the remains can be seen of a swing bridge which once carried a branch of the Midland Railway across the canal into GWR territory at Monk Meadow. The line was completed in 1900 and closed in 1937.

Near to Hempsted Bridge are two single storey warehouses that were built c. 1836 for storing salt. Salt was the principal export cargo from Gloucester and was brought down the river from Droitwich and Stoke Prior in Worcestershire. In the early days two companies maintained stocks ready for any vessel to pick up, but as communications improved, the salt was only brought when required and was loaded directly into the departing ship — often in the Victoria Dock.

To the south of Hempsted Bridge is a small graving dock that was much used for repairing and maintaining barges, lighters and canal longboats.

Nick's timber yard and saw mill with its deserted water frontage